555
Reflections on
GRANDMOTHERS

365
Reflections on
GRANDMOTHERS

Selected and arranged by
Dahlia Porter and Gabriel Cervantes

Adams Media Corporation
Holbrook, Massachusetts

Copyright ©1998, Adams Media Corporation. All rights reserved.
This book, or parts thereof, may not be reproduced in any form
without permission from the publisher; exceptions are made for
brief excerpts used in published reviews.

Published by Adams Media Corporation
260 Center Street, Holbrook, MA 02343

ISBN: 1-55850-811-2

Printed in Canada.

J I H G F E D C B A

Library of Congress Cataloging-in-Publication Data
365 reflections on grandmothers / edited by Dahlia Porter and Gabriel Cervantes.
p.   cm.
Includes bibliographical references.
ISBN 1-55850-811-2 (paperback)
1. Grandmothers—Quotations, maxims, etc. I. Porter, Dahlia. II. Cervantes, Gabriel.
PN6084.G6A16   1997
306.874'5—dc21   97-28115
CIP

This book is available at quantity discounts for bulk purchases.
For information, call 1-800-872-5627 (in Massachusetts, 617-767-8100).

Visit our home page at http://www.adamsmedia.com

for Elsie Parry Porter
my Nain

Contents

❧

Caring

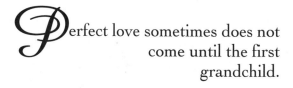

*P*erfect love sometimes does not
come until the first
grandchild.

— *Welsh proverb*

I'm a flower, *poa,* a flower opening and reaching for the sun. You are the sun, grandma, you are the sun in my life.

—*Kitty Tsui*

ne could not live without
delicacy, but when
I think of love I think of the big, clumsy-
looking
hands of my grandmother, each knuckle
a knob.

—*Mona Van Duyn*

*G*randma was a kind of first-aid station, or a Red Cross nurse, who took up where the battle ended, accepting us and our little sobbing sins, gathering the whole of us into her lap, restoring us to health and confidence by her amazing faith in a mortal's strength to meet it.

—*Lillian Smith*

*T*he strength of my conscience came from Grandma, who meant what she said. Perhaps nothing is more valuable for a child than living with an adult who is firm and loving — and Grandma was loving.

—*Margaret Mead*

I went to my grandson and held him. I looked into his piercing, blue eyes. He returned my look with total trust.

— *Charlotte S. Goodhue*

A grandmother proudly wheeled her grandchild into the park. An acquaintance came by, peeked into the carriage and said, "What a gorgeous child!" The grandmother said, "Wait till you see her in pictures."

—*Milton Berle*

*N*o matter what you do, your grandmother thinks it's wonderful.

—*Judith Levy*

*Y*oung people . . . have more compassion and tenderness towards the elderly than most middle-aged adults. Nothing—not avarice, not pride, not scrupulousness, not impulsiveness—so disillusions a youth about her parents as the seemingly inhumane way they treat their grandparents.

—*Louise Kaplan*

*A*s a grandma you are a friend with a special power. You are a friend who can make toast. Better yet, you are a friend who can reach the cookie jar!

—*Leslie Lehr Spirson*

I was an angel in her eyes, no matter what the facts were, no matter what anyone else happened to think.

—*Judy Langford Carter,*
of her grandmother

*B*ecoming a grandparent is a second chance. For you have a chance to put to use all the things you learned the first time around and may have made mistakes on. It's all love and no discipline. There's no thorn in this rose.

—*Dr. Joyce Brothers*

S ome people are ashamed to say 'I'm a grandmother or a grandfather now.' But I have no problem with that because I absolutely love being a grandmother. She is the sweetest thing to happen to me in 17 years. I get to have a baby without all the other trauma.

—*Chaka Khan*

If you think a spanking is not necessary, the chance are you're a grandparent.

—*Evan Esar*

The one thing about Sassy Seats is that grandmothers cannot figure out how they work and are in constant fear of the child's falling. This often makes them forget to comment on other aspects of the child's development, like why he is not yet talking or is still wearing diapers. Some grandmothers will spend an entire meal peering beneath the table and saying, "Is that thing steady?" rather than, "Have you had a doctor look at that left hand?"

—*Anna Quindlen*

*U*ncles, and aunts, and cousins, are all very well, and fathers and mothers are not to be despised; but a *grandmother*, at holiday time, is worth them all.

—*Fanny Fern*

*B*ecoming more flexible, open-minded, having a capacity to deal with change is a good thing. But it is far from the whole story. Grandparents, in the absence of the social institutions that once demanded civilized behavior, have their work cut out for them. Our grandchildren are hungry for our love and approval, but also for standards being set.

—*Eda L. Shan*

When it seems the world can't
understand
Your grandmother's there to hold your
hand.
With her gentle words and open heart.
Your grandmother shares with
graceful art.
Her adoring eyes see just the best
Your grandmother will ignore the rest.
A grandmother's love means
oh, so much!
Your grandmother has that magic touch.

—*Joyce K. Allen Logan*

The bond between grandparents and grandchildren depends on the time they spend alone together and the undivided attention they give to one another.

—*Arthur Kornhaber*

I lived with my grandparents during my high school years. My grandmother worked all her life: caring for other people's children, selling baked goods or Avon products, doing whatever she could to help bring money into the house. She was a beautiful woman, kind and intelligent. She was determined to save my soul.

—*Geoffrey Canada*

grandmother pretends she doesn't know who you are on Halloween.

—*Erma Bombeck*

There often seems to be a playfulness to wise people, as if either their equanimity has as its source this playfulness or the playfulness flows from the equanimity; and they can persuade other people who are in a state of agitation to calm down and manage a smile.

— *Edward Hoagland*

My parents were very young when they had me, and so my grandmother took on a lot of the responsibility of raising me. . . . She gave me direction.

—*Juwan Howard*

*I*f a tooth is loose or someone fell on the playground and scraped their elbow, "Grandma" is always the first to hear about it.

— *Gaye Rizzo*

$\mathcal{M}$any [parents] rush out to buy a cute little baby book to record the meaningful events of our young child's life. . . . But I've often thought there should be a second book, one with room to record the moral milestones of our child's lives. There might be space to record dates she first shared or showed compassion . . . or thought of sending grandma a get-well card or told the truth despite its cost.

—*Fred G. Gosman*

*S*omething magical happens when
parents turn into grandparents.
Their attitude changes from "money-
doesn't-grow-on-trees" to spending it
like it does.

—*Paula Linden*

I hang out with a lot of grandmas. Their grandchildren were all born in mangers and have IQ's so high they cannot be measured. All of them vow that if grandchildren hadn't been invented, we'd have to import them from Japan.

—*Erma Bombeck*

$\mathcal{I}$t's heaven for me; I love it. She had the baby for me. I was thinking about having another one and she beat me to it. It's like I have another kid. It's like I have another baby. . . . I absolutely love being a grandmother. I don't care who knows it.

—*Chaka Khan,*
on becoming a grandmother

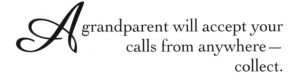

A grandparent will accept your
calls from anywhere—
collect.

—*Erma Bombeck*

*W*hen I work these pieces into cathedral windows, I feel my grandmother's hand guiding me. I'm not sure for whom I'm making this quilt, but it will be someone I love, someone I want to embrace and make warm, even—especially—when we are not near enough to hug or hold each other.

—*Jessica Treadway*

*G*randparents help kids
understand and settle
into a world which can
be pretty confusing
to newcomers.

— *Charles S. Slaybaugh*

$\mathcal{G}$randma comes dragged down
with bags,
hair all awry,
Clean out of breath from puffing up the
road.
She sits and sags
till Mum has stoked her up with tea,
and I sit on her knee
and struggle not to pry
into that interesting load
until she gives the word.
One bulge is bound to be for me. . . .

—*Pam Brown*

A grandmother corrects your
grammar and wipes
imaginary dirt from your cheeks.

—*Sara Spurrier*

The kind sweet souls who love, cherish, inspire and protect their grandchildren are not guardian angels. They are grandmothers.

—*Bettye "Mimi" Flynn*

Grandparents should be one of a child's most valuable resources. They should be gentle teachers of the way life was, and the way it always should be.

—*John Rosemond*

This tiny new granddaughter
Is a thing of wonder
Of beauty.
How perfect her fingers,
Her feathery eyelashes,
Her sweet mouth.
My heart is full to overflowing
As I hold her in my arms,
Touch her cheek with one finger,
Know she will always be
My granddaughter.

— _C. S. Thoni_

Compared to my mother and her friends, with their bobbed hair, knee length dresses from Marshall Field's and high heeled pumps, Grandma looked odd and old-fashioned—like a picture book of Mother Goose rhymes. . . . We loved each other with an unspoken devotion: I was her only grandchild and she was my only living grandparent.

—*Eudora Seyfer*

*T*he grandchildren were always
delighted to see her. . . . They
enjoyed her because she obviously
enjoyed them.

— *Peregrine Churchill,*
grandson of Jennie Jerome Churchill

$\mathcal{I}$'m not a picture taking grandma — but my grandchildren just happen to be the best looking children in the continental United States and you can throw in Canada and the Virgin Islands.

—*Abigail Van Buren*

A grandmother is a woman
who is thrilled because
her grandchild can recite the Gettysburg
Address at eight when Lincoln couldn't
do it until he was much older.

—*Milton Berle*

$\mathcal{M}$y emotions were in turmoil the day my grandson was born. One moment I grinned with joy and pride; my own flesh and blood—my grandson—lay in the nursery, all red-brown and glowing. *This is my grandchild!* I wanted to scream to the world. *See how beautiful he is!*

—*Vickie Noles*

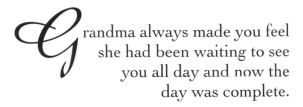

*G*randma always made you feel
she had been waiting to see
you all day and now the
day was complete.

—*Marcy DeMaree*

*T*he quickest way to have
grandparents talk
about their grandchildren is to talk
about yours.

—*Gloria Goldstein*

*T*he true accolade was not only my father saying he would be proud of me, but that my grandmother would have been proud of me.

— *William H. Hastie*

$\mathcal{M}$ost grandparents, like most parents, love their grandchildren unconditionally, regardless of their achievements.

—*Elin McCoy*

*G*randparents are for
wondering
with you.

—*Charlie W. Shedd*

*A*s I grew up . . . what was impenetrable to me was . . . mother's love for her own mother. Between these two there was no generation gap, no chasm. My mother never racked her brains explaining why she and her mother couldn't relate. Lavisa McElroy Loyd was Mama, and all her children felt the same fierce love for her.

—*Shirley Abbott*

Our grandchildren accept us for ourselves, without rebuke or effort to change us, as no one in our entire lives has ever done, not our parents, siblings, spouses, friends—and hardly ever our own grown children.

—*Ruth Goode*

*M*other couldn't wait to pull her grandchildren onto her lap and say, "Let me tell you how rotten your mommy was. She never took naps, and she never picked up her room, and she had a mouth like a drunken sailor in Shanghai. I washed her mouth out with soap so many times I finally had to starch her tongue."

—*Erma Bombeck*

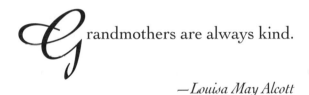

 $\mathscr{G}$randmothers are always kind.

—*Louisa May Alcott*

$\mathcal{L}$et's bring back
grandmothers
—the old fashioned kind, who
take you by the hand and lead you into
the future, safe and savvy and smarter
than your mother.

—*Florence King*

$\mathcal{I}$ could do no wrong in Gramma's eyes. Ever. I think that if I had wound up a serial killer instead of a musician, Gramma would still have loved me.

—*Barry Manilow*

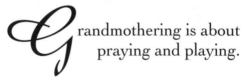

*G*randmothering is about
praying and playing.

—*Anonymous*

The threat of nuclear war and what it could do to my grandchildren's future was more than I could handle. I'll do this work until I can't anymore, or until God says, "Hey, that's enough—come home."

— Trude Britton,
of Grandmothers for Peace

$\mathcal{T}$he bond between child and grandparent can indeed be the purest, least complicated form of human love.

—*Foster W. Cline*

A grandma's lullaby

Little one, precious one,
Time to go off to sleep now,
Hush-a-bye, don't you cry,
Time to go off to Dreamland.
Morning will come and your sunshine
smile
Lights our hearts so sweetly.
Little one, precious one,
Grandma loves you forever.

—*Ann M. Shepard-Simpson*

*G*randmothers can always be
counted on to produce
sweets, cookies and
candies that seem to taste nicer
from her than from anyone else.

—*Elizabeth Faye*

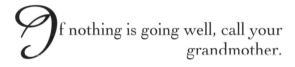

$\mathcal{I}$f nothing is going well, call your grandmother.

—*Italian proverb*

Grandmothers of every race and country have a legendary role as healers: Jewish grandmothers make chicken soup, others have their own special remedies. When a child in a North American Yurok Indian tribe is ill, grandmother goes out into the wilderness to intervene with the spirits by singing and speaking to them. Every grandmother has her own songs.

—*Arthur Kornhaber*

Old-fashioned grandmothers take their grandchildren by the hand and lead them into the future. They are safe and kind, and wiser than the child's mother.

—*Florence King*

A grandam's name is little less
in love
Than is the doting title of a mother.

— *William Shakespeare*

$\mathcal{M}$any times Popo [grandmother] said aloud to all who could hear that my brother and I had fallen out of the bowels of a stupid goose, two eggs that nobody wanted, not even good enough to crack over rice porridge. She said this so that the ghosts would not steal us away. So you see, to Popo we were also very precious.

—*Amy Tan*

A new grandson
Our family
line moves on
How beautiful this day
How wonderful this child
With such shining eyes
And smooth skin.
A new grandson
Brings joy and hope
For a brighter, happier future.

—*C. S. Thoni*

$\mathcal{I}$ could never understand why people were so batty over their grandchildren until mine came into my life. Everything they do, everything they are is precious. I'm looking forward to watching them grow, watching them become.

—Sally Stuart

$\mathcal{I}$ am my mother's, still, I am very much my grandmother's child. I was willed this sense that your elders are your gods on earth. I would have walked behind my grandmother carrying an umbrella if asked.

—*Lisa Jones*

*W*hat luxury grandparents and grandchildren share in the simple enjoyment of each other as people! It has been said that youth is too valuable to waste on children; isn't the quality of grandparenthood so valuable as to be envied?

—*Victoria F. Bumagin*

randmothers don't have to do
anything except be there.

—*Patsy Gray*

*R*apture and euphoria are weak attempts at describing the bliss I felt watching the birth of my granddaughter.

— *Vera Allen-Smith*

[Grandma] would be among the first to express pride at your accomplishments, but she loved us enough to set us straight when we slipped up.

—*Marcy Demaree*

*L*ife is not always perfect, even for grandparents, but . . . the very best part comes when you feel two soft arms around your neck, and you hear the words "I love you, Grandma!"

—Lanie Carter

I didn't expect this child to be such a source of affection. He doesn't give his grandmother one kiss, or even two kisses. Instead, his kisses are a rainforest where the rain never stops falling, little soft kisses on whichever bit of my face is nearest at the moment.

—*Nell Dunn*

I hope my daughter and now my beloved granddaughter, "the pulse and core of my heart," (as the Irish say) have not learned or inherited anything really *bad* from me. I may have spoiled them a bit, but only with love, and I don't believe *real* love does any harm. . . . And how bare my life would have been without them. I'm an old woman now, and can go off happily into the unknown sure that there's a lot of me left behind.

—*Emily Worthington*

Sharing

$\mathcal{I}$n the years since I began
following the ways of
my grandmothers I have come to value
the teachings, stories, and daily
examples of living which they shared
with me. I pity the younger girls of the
future who will miss out on meeting
some of these fine old women.

—*Beverly Hungry Wolf*

$\mathcal{I}$ wouldn't mind our grandchildren thinking of me as a decorative art. Not physically, of course, but in feeling. I am real, I am an actual part of their past, and if I have helped make history more real and alive for them—well, mission accomplished.

—*Dee Hardie*

To be a truly stellar grandparent, I suppose what you do is remember what it was about your own that you loved most, then try to emulate it. My favorite was Oma Hattie, my mother's mother. She taught me how to play gin rummy and canasta. . . . [but] what Oma Hattie taught me (along with card sense) was that when the time came, I should try my best not to be a parent to my grandchildren.

—*Anne Bernays*

I cultivate
Being
Uppity
It's something
My Grandmom taught me.

—*Kate Rushin*

$\mathcal{M}$y grandmother taught me to
believe in miracles.

—*Lilly Mary Vigil*

$\mathcal{A}$nd so our mothers and grandmothers have, more often than not anonymously, handed on the creative spark, the seed of the flower they themselves never hoped to see: or like a sealed letter they could not plainly read . . .

—*Alice Walker*

I write for those who cannot
speak,
voices unrehearsed.
Grandmothers who came before me
whisper silent words —
They are the already born within me
clamoring to be free.
Grandmothers young and old
prod me to tell their stories,
many untold . . .

—*Pauline Brunette Danforth*

It was on these rockers that my mother, her sisters, and my grandmother sat the afternoons of my childhood to tell their stories. . . .

—*Judith Ortiz Cofer*

$\mathcal{M}$y mother and I are still at cross purposes. Particularly since my daughters were born, she whispered in my ear each night as I slept, trying to remake me in her image. I battle her off as well as I can, but she touches me still, and I love her. I would not want my children to grow up without knowing what their grandmother thought.

—*Shirley Abbott*

What I learned from Grandma's stories was this: Women could do hard things and do them competently; problems could be worked out if you ignored what everyone else told you and did what the situation required; sometimes there are men around and sometimes not, but life goes on pretty much the same either way.

—*Sue Hubbell*

$\mathcal{M}$y grandmother's implacable
posture made the idea of
alternatives impossible. What was, was.
Because it had to be.

—*Mary Gordon*

*M*y great-grandmama told my grandmama the past she lived through that my grandmama didn't live through and my grandmama told my mama what they both lived through and my mama told me what they all lived through and we're supposed to pass it down like that from generation to generation so we'll never forget.

— *Gayl Jones*

To our grandchildren, when we tell them about their parent's childhood and young years is living history.

—*Ruth Goode*

I was a sophomore in high school when my grandmother died, and many of my memories of her are from childhood. But when I take out Nana's cookbook, read the notes written in her hand and take her advice on what to cook, she speaks to me again—not as grandmother to child, but as woman to woman, in the language she knew best.

—*Mary Taylor Gray*

A grandmother is a combination of work-worn hands, after a lifetime of toil, a loving heart, and endless stories of the days when her family was young.

—*Elizabeth Faye*

*W*henever our grandchildren are around, the living room at Thornhill becomes center stage. They love to perform. And why not? They have a captive audience for the after-dinner entertainment. By the time the table is cleared, the stage has already been set. Chairs stand in a row, we are given handwritten tickets, and it's the beginning of another show.

—*Dee Hardie*

I never told Grandma how terrified I was because I knew she was not like Mama who always tried to soften the harshness of life for me. I knew Grandma believed in meeting reality head on. She once told me, "Baby, life just ain't fair."

—*Claudia Limbert*

*S*ome of the world's best educators
are grandparents.

—*Charlie W. Shedd*

I'm going to ask something of every one of you. . . . Let me start with my generation—the grandparents out there. You are our living link to the past. Tell your grandchildren the story of the struggle waged, at home and abroad. Of sacrifices freely made for freedom's sake. And tell them your own story as well—because every American has a story to tell.

—*George Bush*

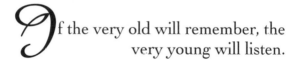

$\mathcal{I}$f the very old will remember, the
very young will listen.

—*Chief Dan George*

$\mathcal{M}$any things I share with my grandmother skipped a generation, from her to me, so they connect us to each other without ever having touched my mother: a taste for rice pudding, an intuition about who is at the other end of a ringing telephone and a tendency to make spontaneous comments that no one quite knows how to respond to. . . .

—*Jessica Treadway*

*W*omen who outlive their
daughters are orphans,
Abuela tells me. Only their
granddaughters can save them, guard
their knowledge like the first fire.

—Christina Garcia

*W*e had an understanding, Grandma and I. She didn't treat me like a child and I didn't treat her like a mother. We played the game by the rules. If I didn't slam her doors and sass, then she didn't spank and lecture me.

—*Erma Bombeck*

Grandparents can be role models about areas that may not be significant to young children directly but that can teach them about patience and courage when we are ill or handicapped by problems of aging. Our attitudes towards retirement, marriage, recreation, even our feelings about death and dying may make much more of an impression than we realize.

—*Eda L. Shan*

*S*o many things we love are you!
I can't seem to explain except
by little things, by flowers and
beautiful hand made things — small
stitches
so much of reading and thinking —
so many sweet customs and so much of
our . . . well, our religion. It is all you.
I hadn't realized it before. This is so
vague but do you see a little, dear
Grandma? I want to thank you.

—*Anne Morrow Lindbergh*

*H*er fearlessness, her public spirit, her contempt for convention, and her indifference to the opinion of the majority have always seemed good to me and have impressed themselves upon me as worthy of imitation.

—*Bertrand Russell,*
of his grandmother

The things that I have instilled in my sons or grandsons or other people around me will live forever. That is me . . .

— *Cecilia Mitchell*

*W*ith both my children and grandchildren I have encouraged them to reach high—not to think about what somebody else is doing about what should be done. And I have always told them that the way to do it is to start with yourself first. And then just spread out.

— *Wendy Watriss*

$\mathscr{O}$ne thing has always stuck in my mind about Grammy—she often says when something's going on she doesn't like. . . .

—*Susan Abbott*

*P*erhaps like many later suffragists, my grandmother was a public feminist and a private isolationist.

—*Gloria Steinem*

I felt as if I was learning a secret, following her fingers in the formula of folds, the choreography of needle on cloth. . . . But the clumsiness of my stitches, compared with my grandmother's graceful ones, frustrated me.

—*Jessica Treadway*

Grandma Faulk persevered against huge odds, and that kind of stubborn dedication to working hard and doing the best you could possibly do was a gift she gave directly to my mother.

—*Diahann Carroll*

I was Grandma's namesake. . . .
She had marked me, she said,
with a mole just above my upper right
lip. She had one in the same spot, so that
as much as justified her insistence that I
bear her name.

—*Deborah E. McDowell*

*B*eing grandparents sufficiently removes us from the responsibilities so that we can be friends—really good friends.

—*Allan Frome*

*W*hen my grandmother . . . hangs up each Saturday night at the end of our long-distance telephone conversation, I always worry that I have left out some critical question: about her dreams and premonitions, her parents' life in New Mexico before it became a state, her memories of herbs, foods and prayers . . . used to cure illness or mark the liturgical seasons. Each conversation is an inheritance; I go into the week feeling whole.

—*Demetria Martinez*

*I*n many parts of the world, grandmothers are considered experts, and a young mother takes it for granted that when she has a question about her baby or needs a little help with him, she'll ask her mother.

—*Benjamin Spock*

It was when you were almost too big to sit in her [grandma's] lap that you began to learn that she was a very special person to talk to. Sometimes, she would give you the right answers without ever saying a word.

—*Harry McMahan*

Family Life

*A*lthough my parents have never been the kind to hint around about grandchildren, I can think of no better tribute to them than giving them some. . . . I can't help thinking that the cycle is not complete until I can introduce them to a child of their child. And I can think of no better comfort when they are gone than to know that something of them lives on, not only in me but in my children.

—*Anne Cassidy*

$\mathcal{I}$f your baby is "beautiful and perfect, never cries or fusses, sleeps on schedule and burps on demand, an angel all the time" . . . you're the grandma.

— *Teresa Bloomingdale*

$\mathcal{W}$e have become a grandmother.

—*Margaret Thatcher*

$\mathscr{I}$t didn't take me long to figure out that one of a grandparent's primary jobs is to always pretend there is very little a child can do that is bothersome.

—*John Rosemond*

dig being a mother . . . and of course, as a grandmother, I just run amok.

— *Whoopi Goldberg*

A mother becomes a true grandmother the day she stops noticing the terrible things her children do because she is so enchanted with the wonderful things her grandchildren do.

—*Lois Wyse*

$\mathcal{N}$o one . . . who has not known the inestimable privilege can possibly realize what good fortune it is to grow up in a home where there are grandparents.

—*Suzanne LaFollette*

*P*arents splitting up, families moving away and fear of old age are just some of the cultural crises that have alienated grandparent from grandchild. . . . It has become harder for grandparents to step into roles taken for granted in the past: as teachers of religion, history and wellness. . . .

—*Demetria Martinez*

The proliferation of support groups suggests to me that too many Americans are growing up in homes that do not contain a grandmother. A home without a grandmother is like an egg without salt and the Helpists know it. They have jumped into the void left by the disappearance of morbid old ladies from the bosom of the American family.

—*Florence King*

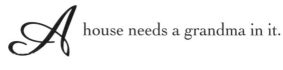

house needs a grandma in it.

—*Louisa May Alcott*

*G*randparents can play a unique role in family life. They can provide the wholehearted nurturance that parents sometimes may be too pressured to give and a sense of history that no textbook can capture. Their light caretaking responsibilities enable them to counsel their grandchildren without passing judgement on youthful passing.

—*Rona Maynard*

*J*ust about the time a woman
thinks her work is done,
she becomes a grandmother.

—*Edward H. Dreschnack*

As I do not live in an age when rustling black skirts billow about me, and I do not carry an ebony stick to strike the floor in sharp rebuke, as this is denied me, I rap out a sentence in my note book and feel better. If a grandmother wants to put her foot down, the only safe place to do it these day is in a note book.

—*Florida Scott-Maxwell*

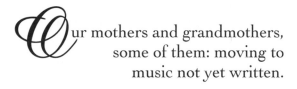

*O*ur mothers and grandmothers,
some of them: moving to
music not yet written.

—*Alice Walker*

She was an aging mother, who fretted over her two adult children, a grandmother, who thought it was her duty to stay up all night overseeing the lives of her eight grown grandchildren. Trouble was, as she saw it (usually, around 4 A.M.) they kept making these *mistakes*.

—*Judith Timson*

A family is a river; some of it
has passed on and more is
to come, and nothing is still, because we
all move along day by day toward our
destination.

—*Dolores Garcia*

Over the river and through the wood,
Now grandmother's cap I spy!
Hurrah for the fun!
Is the pudding done?
Hurrah for the pumpkin pie!

—*Lydia Maria Child,*
from "Thanksgiving Day"

*Y*ou're a much better parent as a grandparent . . . Sartre said he could make his grandmother go into raptures of joy when he was hungry.

—*Arthur Kornhaber*

$\mathcal{E}$rma pulls that "Grandma enjoys it" [Thanksgiving] line on me every year! What enjoyment! What makes all of them think a sixty-five-year old woman likes to get up at 4 A.M., arm-wrestle a naked turkey, stand over a toaster trying to make stale bread into fresh dressing, and spend ten hours making a meal that will take twelve minutes to inhale?

—Erma Bombeck's mother

[*Family*] bonds are formed less by moment of celebration and of crisis than by the quiet, undramatic accretion of minutiae—the remark on the way out of the door, the chore undone, the unexpected smile.

—*George Howe Colt*

lance in the mirror, and you see a person who doesn't "look like a grandparent." But listen to your inner urges and you will find that your "grandparent hunger," your biological need to be a grandparent and to do the best possible job in that vital role, is as insistent as it has been for all people in all places and in all times.

—*Arthur Kornhaber*

*I*f the family were a fruit, it would
be an orange, a circle of sections,
held together but separable — each
segment distinct.

—*Letty Cottin Pogrebin*

$\mathcal{I}$f grandparents want to have a meaningful and constructive role, the first lesson they must learn is that becoming a grandparent is not having a second chance at parenthood!

—*Eda L. Shan*

*H*indered characters
seldom have
mothers
in Irish stories, but they all have
grandmothers.

—*Marianne Moore*

*G*randmotherhood does not give us the right to speak without thinking, but only the right to think without speaking.

—*Lois Wyse*

*M*ost grandparents . . . try hard not to interfere. On the other hand, they have had experience, they feel they've developed judgement, they love their grandchildren dearly, and they can't help having opinions.

—*Benjamin Spock*

$\mathcal{I}$t is strange but true that although we may have learned all sorts of important facts while raising our own children, when we have become grandparents we still tend to forget a whole lot of things we knew.

—*Eda L. Shan*

*G*randmothers are to life what the Ph.D. is to education. There is nothing you can feel, taste, expect, predict, or want that the grandmothers in your family do not know about in detail.

—*Lois Wyse*

To forget one's ancestors is to be a brook without a source, a tree without root.

—*Chinese proverb*

The family the soul wants is a felt
network of relationships, an
evocation of a certain kind of
interconnection that grounds, roots,
and nestles.

— *Thomas More*

$\mathcal{W}$omen must be still as the axis
of a wheel in the midst of her
activities . . . she must be the pioneer in
achieving stillness, not only for her own
salvation, but for the salvation of family
life, of society, perhaps even of
our civilization.

—*Anne Morrow Lindbergh*

earer than our children are the
children of our children.

—Egyptian proverb

By the time Abby Rose was born, I was geared up for the experience. It was one I shall never forget either.

—Isa Kogon,
on the birth of her granddaughter

*N*ever have children, only
grandchildren.

—*Gore Vidal*

*W*hy do grandparents and grandchildren get along so well? They have the same enemy—the Mother!

—*Claudette Colbert*

*B*y the time the youngest children have learned to keep the place tidy, the oldest grandchildren are on hand to tear it to pieces.

—*Christopher Morley*

*Y*ou know, I was really meant
to be a grandmother. It was
mothering that confused
me all of those years.

—*Lois Wyse*

*T*he joy of becoming a mother
was a prelude to the joy of
becoming a grandmother.

— *Vera Allen-Smith*

*W*hen a child is born so are
grandmothers.

—*Judith Levy*

*I*t is as grandmothers that our mothers came into the fullness of their grace. When a man's mother holds his child in her gladden arms he is aware of the roundness of life's cycle; of the mystic harmony of life's ways.

—*Christopher Morley*

*W*hile many of our
grandmothers
led simple lives, some lived simply in the
middle of extraordinary circumstances,
demonstrating great courage, fortitude
and commitment.

— *Valerie Kack-Brice*

he Queen Mother, with a lifetime's popularity, seemed incapable of a bad performance as a national grandmother—warm, smiling, human, understanding, she embodied everything the public could want of its grandmother.

—*John Pearson*

*I*f you close your eyes just for a split second, you can sort of imagine your grandmother made those Pepperidge Farm "Down Home Style Donuts," even though your grandmother is presently a cocktail waitress in Atlantic City.

—*Stephanie Brush*

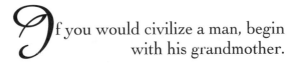

𝓘f you would civilize a man, begin
with his grandmother.

—*Victor Hugo*

I would have liked to go to Ireland, but my grandmother [Queen Victoria] would not let me. Perhaps she thought I wanted to take the little place.

—*German emperor Wilhelm II*

In order not to influence a child,
we must be careful not to be
that child's parent or grandparent.

—*Don Marquis*

*N*ot all of us think grandkids
are the greatest — but that
was before I met mine.

—*Jane Russell*

*T*he need for connection and contact between human beings is very important to acknowledge. Not only do we need intimate relationships with our partners, nuclear families, and close friends, but we also need a sense of connectedness to our extended family, tribe or community. . . . Ultimately, we need to feel we are part of the whole human society and connected to all beings on earth.

—*Shakti Gawain*

$\mathcal{L}$et's bring back grandmothers!
It's time Americans stopped
worrying about *interference* and being a
burden on the children and regrouped
under one roof.

—*Florence King*

Grandchildren are more
tolerant of you than
their parents are.
Maybe it's because they have to put up
with your foibles for a shorter
span of time.

—*Celestine Sibley*

$\mathcal{Y}$our sons weren't made to like you. That's what grandchildren are for.

—*Jane Smiley*

Sons forget what grandsons wish
to remember.

—*Alice Rossi*

The pairing of young and old creates an openness not always found in adult relationships.

—*Suzanne Larronde*

*A*ll elders should have at least one youngster to be "crazy about" and vice versa. Grandparenting supplies the role model for a healthy and fulfilling old age. And grandchildren want grandparents.

—Arthur Kornhaber

*I*t's such a grand thing to be a
mother of a mother—that's
why the world calls her grandmother.

—*Anonymous*

*M*y mother had no dreams to lay on my children. She had tried . . . and succeeded . . . and failed with my sister and me. She was done with that now and her grandsons couldn't defeat her. Or disappoint her. Or prove anything—anything good or bad—about her. And I saw her free of ambition, free of the need to control, free of anxiety. Free, as she put it—to enjoy.

—Judith Viorst

Wow! Are grandchildren great!
Spoil them rotten—give
them back—and laugh and laugh.
Revenge is sweet.

—*Aris Painter*

A grandmother is a baby-sitter
who watches the kids
instead of the television.

—Anonymous

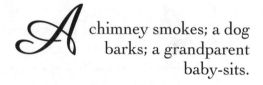

A chimney smokes; a dog barks; a grandparent baby-sits.

—*Edwina Sherudi*

*B*y the time a couple can afford to go out evenings, they have to babysit with the grandchildren.

—*Evan Esar*

*G*randchildren don't make a
man feel old; it's the
knowledge that he's
married to a grandmother.

—*G. Norman Collie*

The thrill of being a
grandmother,
however, pales next to the ecstasy of
being a great-grandmother.

—*Beatrice L. Cole*

*I*f I'd known how wonderful it
would be to have
grandchildren, I'd have had them first.

—*Anonymous grandmother*

They say genes skip generations.
Maybe that's why
grandparents find their grandchildren
so likeable.

—*Joan McIntosh*

When grandparents enter the
door, discipline flies out
the window.

—*Ogden Nash*

One grandmother will spoil a baby. Two working together will bring him up in the way he should go, for each will suspect the other of spoiling him and will check it.

— *William Allen White*

The purpose of discipline is self-discipline, and its best source is the full-time hovering presence of a grandmother. Grandmothers don't spoil children, tired parents do.

—*Florence King*

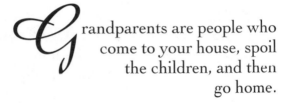

*G*randparents are people who
come to your house, spoil
the children, and then
go home.

—*Anonymous*

*I*f grandmas hadn't existed, kids would have inevitably invented them.

—*Arthur Kornhaber*

What's so simple even a small
child can manipulate it?
Why, a grandmother, of course!

—*Anonymous*

*F*amilies will not be broken. Curse and expel them, send their children wandering, drown them in flood and fires, and old women will make songs out of all these sorrows and sit on the porches and sing them on mild evenings.

—Marilynne Robinson

The only thing that endures is that line, the people who can't be changed, exchanged, substituted for.

—*Marilyn French*

The presence of a grandparent confirms that parents were, indeed, little once, too, and that people who are little can grow to be big, can become parents and one day even have grandchildren of their own. So often we think of grandparents as belonging to the past; but in this important way, grandparents, for young children, belong to the future.

—*Fred Rogers*

The closest friends I have made
all through life have been
people who also grew up close to a loved
and loving grandmother or grandfather,

—*Margaret Mead*

You will learn more about the American family from 10 randomly chosen grandmothers than you will from 10 randomly chosen family experts.

—*David Blankenhorn*

*G*randma was the heart of this family. Her love and support were total and unconditional.

—*Marcy DeMaree*

*I*n peasant communities where things didn't change and where people died in the beds they were born in, grandparents taught the young what the end of life was going to be. So you looked at your mother, if you were a girl, and learned what it was like to be a bride, a young mother. Then you looked at your grandmother and you knew what it was like to be old. [Children] ... were prepared for the end of life at the beginning.

—*Margaret Mead*

*M*om still sends me money. Out of her Social Security check she sends money to children, grandchildren, and great-grandchildren. We send it back—on Mother's Day, on birthdays, at Christmas. Do we have a family that works? I hope so.

—*Kim Williams*

Generations

$\mathcal{S}$oon I will be an old, whitehaired lady, into whose lap someone places a baby, saying, "Smile, Grandma!" — I, who myself so recently was photographed on my grandmother's lap.

—Liv Ullmann

*G*randmas shed the yoke of responsibility, relax, and enjoy their grandchildren in a way that was not possible when they were raising their own children. And they can glow in the realization that here is the seed of life that will harvest generations to come.

—*Erma Bombeck*

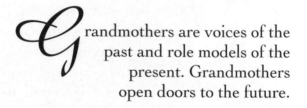

*G*randmothers are voices of the
past and role models of the
present. Grandmothers
open doors to the future.

—*Helen Ketchum*

*A*nother appealing aspect to having grandparents is that they do help to give [your child] a sense of continuity—of his place in the world and in the generations. Not only do grandparents help him intellectually to comprehend that there are parents of parents, but they also aid him in understanding where he fits in the successions of things. Even a very young child can begin to feel a sense of rootedness and history.

—*Lawrence Balter*

$\mathcal{T}$he people whom the sons and daughters find it hardest to understand are the fathers and mothers, but young people can get on very well with the grandfathers and grandmothers.

—*Simeon Strunsky*

$\mathcal{I}$t was a quilt begun by his grandmother and finished by his mother and his aunt. He had stared at it when he was a child: squares of different sizes, alternately light and dark —a diamond pattern radiating from the smallest gray square in the center.

—*Ann Beattie*

*R*emembering my grandmother connects me to the human continuum that endures amidst change. She reminds me that I'm not only myself, spawned and existing in the present, but one link in the chain of ongoing generations.

—*Robin Reif*

*O*n a trunk in my attic is a white dress my grandmother wore to suffrage marches when she was in college. . . . The neckline, cuffs, belt, and front panel had been embroidered by my great-grandmother with satin-stitch flowers. The white dress lay in the middle of a stack that began with corsets and bustle skirts and ended with a denim miniskirt embroidered with psychedelic flowers.

—*Kathleen Kilgore*

My grandmother opens her
mouth
and her mother awakes.
We are wrapped in one
rainbow shawl.
Somewhere hidden,
their words whispered as snow
held in the sky.

—*Mary Freericks*

$\mathcal{W}$e all grow up with the weight of history on us. Our ancestors dwell in the attics of our brains as they do in the spiraling chains of knowledge hidden in every cell of our bodies.

—*Shirley Abbott*

$\mathcal{I}$t's an unlikely treasure—its binding cracked, its back broken, its covers frayed. But between these worn covers [of Nana's cookbook] is something priceless—a link to my grandmother, my childhood, my family.

—*Mary Taylor Gray*

*S*he said there were two people you had to be true to—those people that came before you and those people who came after you.

—*Gayl Jones*

I had trouble placing my grandmother's house. I knew it had nothing to do with America. Or postwar life. And yet it stood at the center of the lives of all her children and her children's children. It expressed an era—ahistorical, perhaps wholly imaginary—that we grandchildren vaguely understood.

—*Mary Gordon*

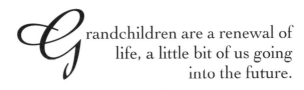

$\mathcal{G}$randchildren are a renewal of
life, a little bit of us going
into the future.

—Helene Schellenberg Barnhart

$\mathcal{M}$y eyes misted at the sight of my granddaughter handling her own child. Not too long ago I had stood this way and watched my daughter doing the same things with Dena [my granddaughter].

—*Betty Baum*

*S*arah Mahan spelled it out in her bequest: "This quilt . . . I give & bequeath unto her sister . . . or . . . otherwise to the oldest granddaughter of their father. . . ." Sarah was putting into words what so many quiltmakers felt: that the female family — past, present and future — was important, and that these generations were united by the quilts that were the work of their hands and hearts.

— *Ricky Clark*

I look at my hands, Momma
And I see yours
And those of your mother before you.

—Laura Davis

$\mathcal{D}$id Great-grandma Glenda know when she stitched all those pieces together that someday her great-granddaughter would lie awake under the quilt, tossing and turning and worrying? When she sewed it, she probably didn't think twice about her own children, let alone about her great-grandchildren. Probably she was thinking about her new husband and what they'd do under the quilt.

—*Jocelyn Riley*

An accurate charting of the American woman's progress through history might look more like a corkscrew tilted slightly to one side, its loops inching closer to the line of freedom with the passage of time—but like a mathematical curve approaching infinity, never touching its goal. . . . Each time, the spiral turns her back just short of the finish line.

—*Susan Faludi*

*W*hen grandma was a girl she
didn't do things the girls
do today. But then the grandmas didn't
do things grandmas do today.

—*Anonymous*

The very fact that you don't look or act or feel like the grandparents of even a generation ago does not mean that you are less, but that you are more—in effect, an evolved form of grandparents, primed to do a bigger and more challenging job than any group before you.

—*Arthur Kornhaber*

*T*he next generation of women
will enter a world in which
they are perceived to have more
opportunities for creating fulfilling lives
than women have ever had before.

—*Elizabeth Debold,
Idelisse Malaye, and Marie Wilson*

*I*n case you're worried about what's going to become of the younger generation, it's going to grow up and start worrying about the younger generation.

—*Roger Allen*

*E*very generation must go further
than the last or what's the use
in it?

—*Meridel Le Sueur*

*E*ven very recently, the elders could say: "You know, I have been young and you never have been old." But today's young people can reply: "You never have been young in the world I am young in, and you never can be." . . . This break between generations is wholly new: it is planetary and universal.

—*Margaret Mead*

Each generation's job is to question what parents accept as faith, to explore possibilities, and to adapt the last generation's system of values for a new age.

— *Frank Pittman*

*I*t is important for the elders to be willing to give wisdom and not to try to direct everything. Young people see themselves living in this world and it is their life yet to be lived.

—*Maya Angelou*

*S*ome people are your relatives but others are your ancestors, and you choose the ones you want to have as ancestors. You create yourself out of those values.

—*Ralph Ellison*

Each generation supposes that the
world was simpler for the one
before it.

—Eleanor Roosevelt

Great-grandmother had no movies, no automobile, no airplanes, no radios; is it any wonder she wove her pleasure into patchwork quilts?

— *Carrie A. Hall and Rose G. Kretsinger*

*I*n every age "the good old days" were a myth. No one ever though they were good at the time. For every age has consisted of crises that seemed intolerable to the people that lived through them.

—*Brooks Atkinson*

*H*istory never looks like history
when you are living through
it. It always looks confusing and messy,
and it always feels uncomfortable.

—*John W. Gardner*

*W*ithin your own generation —
the same songs, the same
wars, the same attitudes towards those
wars, the same rules and radio shows in
the air — you can gauge the possibilities
and impossibilities. With a person of
another generation, you are treading
water, playing with fire.

—*John Updike*

*E*very age and generation must be as free to act for itself in all cases as the ages and generations which preceded it.

— *Thomas Paine*

When three generations are
present in a family, one
of them is bound to be revolutionary.

—*Elise Boulding*

*W*e didn't have a generation
gap, we had a generation
Grand Canyon.

—Mary Crow Dog

*B*ecause [grandparents] are usually free to love and guide and befriend the young without having to take daily responsibility for them, they can often reach out past pride and fear of failure and close the space between generations.

—*Jimmy Carter*

*T*oday age segregation has passed all sane limits. Not only are fifteen-year-olds isolated from seventy-year-olds but social groups divide those in high school from those in junior high, and those who are twenty from those who are twenty-five. There are middle-middle-age groups, late-middle-age groups, and old-age groups—as though people with five years between them could not possibly have anything in common.

—*Suzanne Gordon*

The linking of generations, the
historical lineage of family,
the sharing of love . . . give
purpose to life.

— *George Landberg*

*A*ncestral habits of mind can be constricting; they also confer one's individuality.

—*Bharati Mukherjee*

*B*ecause you are a grandparent,
you are wise and experienced
in the eyes of a small child. You are the
voices of times past.

—*Linda B. White*

There is a delight, a comfort, an easing of the burden, a renewal of joy in my own life, to feel the stream of life of which I am part going on like this.

—*Betty Friedan,*
on being a grandmother

randchildren are the dots that
connect the lines from
generation to generation.

—*Lois Wyse*

It's safe to say that my grandmother never envisioned that she would have a granddaughter one day . . . and this granddaughter would have her own money, can shop—50 percent off, full price, doesn't matter, she never has to ask anyone's permission—because she makes her own living, doing what is important to her, which is to tell stories, many of them about her grandmother. . . .

—*Amy Tan*

$\mathcal{F}$or what is the worth of human life,
unless it is woven into the life of
our ancestors by the records of history.

—*Cicero*

These remarkable women of olden times are like the ancient painted glass—the art of making them is lost; my mother was less than her mother, and I am less than my mother.

—*Harriet Beecher Stowe*

In a brief space the generations of living beings are changed and like runners pass on the torches of life.

—*Lucretius*

*G*randparents impart history and values by their existence; it made the existence of their grandchildren possible.

— *Robert A. Aldrich and Glenn Austin*

Grandparents are always being told that they are living history to their grandchildren, that they give the children the reassurance of their roots. For me and many grandmothers I have talked to, it works the other way as well. They give *us* continuity.

—*Ruth Goode*

*H*eredity is an absorbing study — our forbears live in us and bear their part in all we do. This gives me a fresh zest for living when I look at my own grandchildren and see the thrill of life that was in that older generation, reflected in them.

— *Sybil Thorndike Casson*

When I first saw my grandchild I was bursting with joy and pride. I'd never had a feeling quite like that before . . . to see your own child produce another child and to know that it came through you. It was a wonder, a mystery, and there was something else, too—a wonder of nature.

—*Anonymous*

*H*olding these babies in my arms
makes me realize the miracle
my husband and I began.

—Betty Ford,
of her grandchildren

$\mathcal{S}$eeing a child as one's grandchild
one can visualize that same
child as a grandparent, and with the
eyes of another generation, one can see
other children . . . who must be taken
into account — now.

—*Margaret Mead*

Age

A grandmother is a little girl
who suddenly shows up
one day with a touch of gray in her hair.

—*Harry McMahan*

$\mathcal{I}$ think of age as a great universalizing force. It's the only thing we all have in common. It doesn't begin when you collect your social security benefits. Aging begins with the moment of birth, and it ends only when life itself has ended. Life is a continuum; only, we—in our stupidity and blindness—have chopped it up into little pieces and kept all those pieces separate.

—*Maggie Kuhn*

To Angela her grandmother was old but had not grown older and was never younger. This is a usual way with grandmothers.

—*Cynthia Propper Seton*

When I was a child . . . I would think it must be marvelous to issue those proclamations of experience — "It was at least ten years ago" or "I hadn't seen him for twenty years." But chronological prestige is tenacious: once attained, it can't be shed; it increases moment by moment, day by day, pressing its honors on you until you are lavishly, overly endowed with them.

—*Shirley Hazzard*

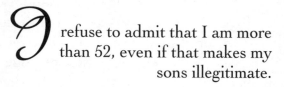

I refuse to admit that I am more than 52, even if that makes my sons illegitimate.

—*Nancy Astor*

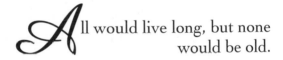

*A*ll would live long, but none
would be old.

—*Benjamin Franklin*

I am very pleased with each advancing year. It stems back to when I was forty. I was a bit upset about reaching that milestone, but an older friend consoled me. 'Don't complain about growing old—many people don't have that privilege.'

—*Earl Warren*

*W*ho could ask for anything more than a pride of half a dozen grandchildren to keep us young?

—Dee Hardie

𝒥t's never too late to have a fling
For autumn is just as nice as
spring
And it's never too late to fall in love.

—Sandy Wilson

The years that a woman subtracts for her age are not lost. They are added to the ages of other women.

—Diane de Poitiers

*O*f Time thought no more of me, than I do of Time, I believe I should bid defiance, for one while, to old age and wrinkles, — for deuce take me if ever I think about it all.

—Fanny Burney

$\mathcal{I}$n youth we learn; in age we understand.

—*Marie von Ebner Eschenbach*

 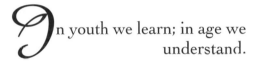

$\mathcal{N}$othing really matters but living—accomplishments are the ornaments of life, they come second.

— *Willa Cather*

The older I get, the greater power I seem to have to help the world; I am like a snowball—the further I am rolled the more I gain.

—*Susan B. Anthony*

*C*ome, Captain Age,
    With your sea-
chest full of treasure!
Under the yellow and wrinkled
    tarpaulin
Disclose the carved ivory
And the sandalwood inlaid with pearl:
Riches of wisdom and years.

—*Sarah Norcliffe Cleghorn*

I have learned little from the years that fly; but I have wrung the color from the years.

—*Frances Pollock*

There are compensations for growing older. One is the realization that to be sporting isn't at all necessary. It is a great relief to reach this stage of wisdom.

—*Cornelia Otis Skinner*

$\mathcal{K}$in refused to forget her
femininity.
Death itself was preferable to the
blowsiness of the average old woman.
There was a poem — composed, they
said, by
some famous woman of the past —
Never could human form
Aspire, I know,
To beauty ripe as that now bends
This rose. Yet, somewhere here,
I see myself.

—*Hayashi Fumiko*

"*Age ain't nothin' but a number.*" But age is other things, too. It is wisdom, if one has lived one's life properly. It is experience and knowledge. And it is getting to know all the ways the world turns, so that if you cannot turn the world the way you want, you can at least get out of the way so you won't get run over.

—*Miriam Makeba*

*N*o Spring, nor Summer beauty
hath such grace,
As I have seen in one Autumnal face.

—*John Donne*

While grandma looks forward to special moments with her grandchild, she must now schedule those moments in between her other engagements, like working, working out, and being worked over (nails and hair).

—*Paula Linden*

*L*et us respect gray hairs,
especially our own.

—*J. P. Senn*

I have always felt that a woman has the right to treat the subject of her age with ambiguity until, perhaps, she passes into the realm of over ninety. Then it is better she be candid with herself and with the world.

—*Helena Rubinstein*

"*A*ge" is the acceptance of a term of years. But maturity is the glory of years.

—Martha Graham

With age, we become responsible for what's in our heads—the character of the memories there, the music we are familiar with, the storehouse of books we have read, the people we can call, the scenery we know and love. Our memories become our dreams.

—*Edgar Hoagland*

*O*ld places and old persons in their turn, when spirits dwell in them, have an intrinsic vitality of which youth is incapable; precisely the balance and wisdom that comes from long perspectives and broad foundations.

—*George Santayana*

Age. Ageism. In a society rooted in a virtual cult to youth, the nature and circumstance of youth is often grossly distorted. But the nature of age is often invisible.

—*Margaret Randall*

You can only perceive real
beauty in persons as
they get older.

—*Anouk Aimée*

$\mathcal{A}$ letter from a lady who has described me in a French newspaper — 'a noble lady with a shock of white hair' — Lord, are we as old as all that? I feel about six and a half.

—*Virginia Woolf,*
to Vanessa Bell

Even very young grandparents seem enormously old to a small child, although the child may politely deny it. One small girl, feeling proud of reaching the monumental age of four, turned to her young-looking grandmother and asked, "How come I'm so old if you're so new?"

—*Alison Judson Ryerson*

How old would you be if you
didn't know how old
you are?

—*Satchel Paige*

I have enjoyed greatly the second blooming that comes when you finish the life of emotions and of personal relations; and suddenly you find—at the age of fifty, say—that a whole new life has opened before you, filled with things you can think about, study, or read about, . . . It is as if a fresh sap of ideas and thoughts was rising in your head.

—*Agatha Christie*

$\mathcal{N}$ature gives you the face you have at twenty; it is up to you to merit the face you have at fifty.

—*Coco Chanel*

$\mathscr{I}$ grasped her hand like a common consoling friend and felt, immediately, the grim forbidding strength of her, undiminished all these years.

—*Louise Erdrich,*
of her grandmother

We grow neither better nor
worse as we get old, but
more like ourselves.

—*May Lamberton Becker*

*A*ge is opportunity no less
Than youth itself,
though in another dress,
And as the evening twilight fades away
The sky is filled with stars.

—*Henry Wadsworth Longfellow*

*A*ge is something that doesn't
matter, unless you
are a cheese.

—*Billie Burke*

*Y*ou must learn day by day, year by year, to broaden your horizon. The more things you love, the more you are interested in, the more you enjoy, the more you are indignant about—the more you have left when anything happens.

—*Ethel Barrymore*

$\mathcal{W}$e are always the same
age inside.

—*Gertrude Stein*

The hey-day of a woman's life is on the shady side of fifty, when the vital forces heretofore expended in other ways are garnered in the brain, when thoughts and sentiments flow out in broader channels, when philanthropy takes the place of selfishness, and when from the depths of poverty and suffering the wail of humanity grows as pathetic to the ears as once was the cry of their own children.

—*Elizabeth Cady Stanton*

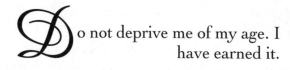

*D*o not deprive me of my age. I
have earned it.

—*May Sarton*

*I*f becoming a grandmother was only a matter of choice I would advise every one of you straight away to become one. There is no fun for old people like it!

—*Hannah Withall Smith*

To keep the heart unwrinkled, to be hopeful, kindly, cheerful, reverent — that is to triumph over old age.

— *Thomas Bailey Aldrich*

$\mathcal{H}$er grandmother, as she got older, was not fading but rather becoming more concentrated.

—*Paulette Bates Alden*

There is a case for keeping wrinkles. They are the long-service stripes earned in the hard campaign of life.

—Daily Mail,
London editorial

*M*y grandmother started walking five miles a day when she was sixty. She's ninety-seven now, and we don't know where the hell she is.

—*Ellen DeGeneres*

I'm 65 and I guess that puts me in the geriatrics. But if there were 15 months in every year, I'd only be 48. That's the trouble with us. We number everything. Take women, for example. I think they deserve to have more than twelve years between 28 and 40.

—*James Thurber*

*T*he great thing about getting
    older is that you don't lose
all the other ages that you have been.

—*Madeleine L'Engle*

From the earliest times the old have rubbed it into the young that they are wiser than they, and before the young had discovered what nonsense this was they were too old, and it profited them to carry on the imposture.

— *W. Somerset Maugham*

$\mathcal{W}$e turn not older with years,
but newer every day.

—Emily Dickinson

*A*ging calls us outdoors, after the adult indoors or work and love-life and keeping stylish, into the lovely simplicities that we thought we had outgrown as children. We come out again to love the plain world, its stone and wood, its air and water.

—*John Updike*

*S*ome of the things which seemed crucial and of earth-shaking importance when you were raising your children have had the chaff sifted out of them by the years and you can recognize that they are of minor, even trivial, size.

—*Celestine Sibley*

$\mathcal{W}$hat could be more beautiful
than a dear old lady
growing wise with age?

—*Brigitte Bardot*

*T*he wrinkles aren't exactly pretty but they are—well, dear. . . . If I managed to eradicate them . . . would my face be as unmistakably mine?

—*Susan Jacoby*

*L*ong after I have forgotten all
my human loves, I shall still
remember the smell of a gooseberry leaf,
or the feel of wet grass on my bare feet.
In the long run, it is this feeling that
makes life worth living.

— *Gwen Raverat*

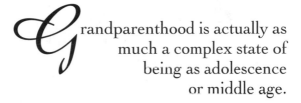

Grandparenthood is actually as
much a complex state of
being as adolescence
or middle age.

—*Edwina Sherudi*

As I've gotten older, I've gotten more sure of myself. I was a shy and withdrawn young mother; and I am not a shy and withdrawn grandmother.

—*Berniece Rooke*

She seems to have had the ability to stand firmly on the rock of her past while living completely and unregretfully in the present.

—*Madeleine L'Engle*

*M*y grandmother is over eighty
and still doesn't need
glasses. Drinks right out of the bottle.

—*Henny Youngman*

*W*hat in heaven's name is so strange about a grand-mother dancing nude? I bet lots of grandmothers do it.

—*Sally Rand*

$\mathcal{G}$randmother, about eighty, is visiting in the East and sends home things she has bought for her house. "I don't suppose I shall live forever," she says, "but while I do live I don't see why I shouldn't live as if I expected to."

—*Charles Horton Cooley*

*W*e all know grandparents whose values transcend passing fads and pressures, and who possess the wisdom of distilled pain and joy.

—*Jimmy Carter*

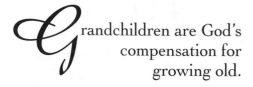

$\mathcal{G}$randchildren are God's
compensation for
growing old.

—*Anonymous*

$\mathcal{G}$randmas of the 90's have been restyled. . . . Closets once filled with flowered dresses and sensible shoes have been replaced by spandex and Reeboks.

—*D. L. Stewart*

Even now I am not old. I never think of it, and yet I am a grandmother to eleven grandchildren. I also have seventeen great-grandchildren.

—Anna Mary Moses,
better known as Grandma Moses

*S*uddenly I wasn't so afraid of growing old and wrinkled. I saw that one day, if I was really lucky, I just might qualify to be someone's superlatively soft and cuddly grandmother.

—*Noelle Fintushel*

I tried hard to be cool about the looming first grandchild — the first of five boys — but my unconscious tricked me into reading the nameplate on a Pontiac as "Grand Ma" when it was clearly "Grand Am."

—*Anne Bernays*

The advantage of being eighty
years old is that one has had
many people to love.

—*Jean Renoir*

'Tis well to give honour and glory
to Age,
With its lessons of wisdom and truth;
Yet who would not go back to the
fanciful page,
And the fairytale read but in youth?

—*Eliza Cook*

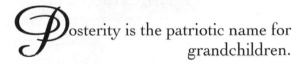

osterity is the patriotic name for grandchildren.

—*Art Linkletter*

$\mathcal{T}$he oddities of shape that age has
given me,
defeating exercise and diet,
making me appear hump-backed, pot-bellied,
flabby-armed
when inside in reality I am slim and straight
and, bracing all my muscles,
prove to be purpose-built
for carting grandchildren from place to place.
I am a breathing, ambulatory armchair
the perfect place for cuddles.

—*Pam Brown*

I am rich with years, a millionaire! I have been part of my own generation, then I watched my children's generation grow up, then my grandchildren's, and now my great-grandchildren's.

—*Dolores Garcia*

Memories

I remember my grandmother wrapping fifteen cents in the corner of an envelope, tying it with a rubber band, and throwing it down from the third floor so I could buy rainbow-colored ices in paper cups from the man in the white truck.

—*Dorothy Greenbaum*

$\mathcal{M}$y Mamá Grande, a tiny Mayan woman, took me aside when I was an adolescent and told me several things that didn't make a bit of sense to my young and inattentive ears, and as young people tend to waste all attempts of our elders to relay to us wisdom accumulated over the decades, I thought my Mamá Grande had a few mice in the attic.

—*Ana Castillo,*
of her grandmother

$\mathcal{I}$ loved their home. Everything smelled older, worn but safe; the food aroma had baked itself into the furniture.

—*Susan Strasberg,*
of her grandparent's home

I can still see Nana after Sunday dinner
trying to divide her lemon meringue pie
into nine perfectly equal pieces.

—*J. Fairweather Hughes*

We danced on and on, unequal partners who in those moments absolutely loved all the inequalities about us, the jokiness, the seriousness. My grandmother was singing: her voice was loud and clear. She spun me for a long time. Our heads thrown back, legs stepping, arms pumping, our fingers intertwined.

—*Marcie Hershman*

I always gathered
Spring greens
with Gram
down by Mission Creek.

—Sheryl L. Nelms

$\mathcal{G}$randma had an almost
magical talent of
making something out
of nothing. Not only did she preserve
every scrap of food she could for our
hard winters, but she was a forager
before it became fashionable.

— *Claudia Limbert*

*L*et nothing go to waste—that was one of grandmother's rules.

—*Jilann Sevenson*

*H*elped Grandma with the weekend shopping. She was dead fierce in the grocers; she watched the scales like a hawk watching a fieldmouse. Then she pounced and accused the shop assistant of giving her underweight bacon. The shop assistant was dead scared of her and put another slice on.

—*Sue Townsend*

*G*randma was a heavy, big-boned woman. Her face was pleasant with smile-wrinkles fanning out from the corners of her pale blue eyes, but she was plain, and because she believed lipstick and rouge were sinful, she did nothing to enhance her appearance.

—*Eudora Seyfer*

I know exactly what Grandma
would
think of this. I know how she
hung her washing, Monday mornings
early, every piece just so, grouped
by purpose, color, size, down the
long lines stretched from house to barn.

—*Rebecca Baggett*

*W*e girls spent sultry afternoons trying to tame her cats. We didn't have to worry about what to call them or how to tell them apart. They were all calicoes, and Grandma named every one of them Minnie.

— *Teresa Wendel*

$\mathcal{M}$y grandmother remembers
with her heart those
tender childhood moments that I have
long forgotten.

—*Joyce K. Allen Logan*

*I*t was dramatic to watch my grandmother decapitate a turkey with an ax the day before Thanksgiving. Nowadays the expense of hiring grandmothers for the ax work would probably qualify all turkeys so honored with "gourmet" status.

—*Russell Baker*

*G*randma would grab the
shotgun and race to
the henhouse when
she heard sounds of a weasel raid.

—*Claudia Limbert*

*S*omething about grandmother is always making you hungry. Maybe it's the apple pies baking and the chicken frying and the biscuits in the oven. But Grandma always has the nicest smelling house.

—*Harry McMahan*

*G*randma's biscuits were as big
as our hands. She didn't cut
them, she pinched off a
handful of dough and patted and shaped
it like a small loaf. Nobody's biscuits
tasted like Grandma's.

—*Martha Kezer Merideth*

While Margaret Sargent was alive, I only knew her as my grandmother, though she was always an unconventional one. . . . I was always told she was an artist, but there were none of her paintings in our house, so I thought the description must have something to do with why she sent me a green satin evening bag when I was eleven; her use of odd colored inks; or her scandalous love affairs with both women and men.

—*Honor Moore*

*M*y grandmother was nice to me. She loved me and my sister, too. We slept all three in the same bed. . . . My grandmother cooked pasta—every night pasta, every night. I ate pasta fagioli and pasta with cauliflower and pasta with broccoli, pasta with lentils and every night she changed the pasta.

—*Michelena Gaetano Profeta*

$\mathcal{G}$randma Gottfried never expressed much of a liking for anyone, but she appeared to have the least amount of ill will toward the Chihuahua.

—*Davida Rosenblum*

*N*anny never missed a night looking under the bed before she got in it. She said she wanted to make sure there wasn't a man under there. I always thought if there was, she'd scare him more than he'd scare her because she wore long underwear with a drop seat that sagged and her teeth were out.

— *Carol Burnett*

$\mathcal{M}$y very first feeling on looking at my grandson's face took me aback. It was as if neither of us were present, as if I for a second lost myself and couldn't find him in some ineffable void. No feeling of recognition or of his belonging to me in any way. As I came to, my first articulated feeling was actually one of respect for him.

—*Anne Truitt*

$\mathcal{G}$randchildren provide us with some of our proudest occasions, some of our tenderest experiences, and, without question, some of the funniest moments.

—*Catharine Brandt*

*M*ary's son was born early this morning. After hearing the news I lay back in the predawn dark and, as the tide of happiness receded, I saw that it had pulled out on some long, bare inner shoreline of myself and had make the slope glisten for the last time: both my daughters were now mothers and in the proper nature of things more mothers of their children than they are daughters of their mother.

—*Anne Truitt*

Whenever I feel myself inferior to everything about me, threatened by my own mediocrity . . . I can still hold up my head and say to myself: "Let me not forget that I am the daughter of a woman who bent her head, trembling, between the blades of a cactus, her wrinkled face full of ecstasy over the promise of a flower, a woman who herself never ceased to flower, untiringly, during three quarters of a century."

—*Colette*

*Y*our hands are trembling,
and your face is
wrinkled
delicately.
The white hair on your cheek
quivers as you sleep,
Grandmother.

—*Lisa Williams*

$\mathcal{M}$y grandmother was a very tough woman. She buried three husbands. Two of them were napping.

—*Rita Rudner*

There was always company at my grandmother's Sunday dinner table: relatives or a visiting evangelist, deacons of the church, a delegation from the Ladies' Aid Society, Kenneth from the Home for the Blind, or a spinster waif.

—*Joyce Butler*

I was her little shadow, and that was just the way I wanted it. Googy was two hundred years old and would let me chase her all around the big old house and tickle her. When I caught her, I didn't tickle her too hard because she could have broken.

Carol Burnett,
of her grandmother

*S*he'd had her fortune told, her palm read, from time to time, the tarot. It was a comfort and she wasn't going to stop it. Not for a bunch of uppity know-it-alls. Gram sometimes seemed like the child of her daughters, the bad and willful one they couldn't do a thing with but loved the best because of her charm and daring.

—*Joan Chase*

It happens every spring. Perhaps there is something about the way the sunlight strikes the land, as though coming through a great expanse of green water; perhaps it is the promising smell of the earth, damp from melted snow. Every spring I am back in the 1940's with Grandma and her chickens.

— *Claudia Limbert*

*G*oing to see my grandparents
was the highlight of my
childhood summers. . . .
I was doted upon, admired, entertained
and overfed. I was never more content
and happy.

— *Carolyn Anthony*

$\mathcal{M}$y grandmother had no interest in having a good time—that is, in doing anything that would result only in pleasure—and her house proclaimed this, as it proclaimed everything about her. Her house was her body and, like her body, was honorable, daunting, reassuring, defended, castigating, harsh, embellished, dark.

—*Mary Gordon*

*J*ust as in Grandfather's courtroom, many women also gathered in my grandmother's domain, the kitchen, to pour out their troubles and joys, to voice their problems and difficulties.

—*Isaac Bashevis Singer*

It wasn't that Nai-Nai was adverse to change; she was merely impervious to it. External events might jostle her composure a bit, but her core was rock solid and immutable.

—*Leslie Li*

*T*here isn't anything more positive in my life than my grandmother. . . . I saw my mom and my grandmother go to work every day. I didn't know until I was an adult that there were different jobs for women and men. They never complained. To them, there was dignity in work. They were proud. Proud that they were never on welfare, and that they provided for their family.

—*Georgette Mosbacher*

I loved my grandmother more than any other human being because she never lied, never told you what you wanted to hear, never compromised. She had a healthy hatred for all living human beings, all systems of government, all religion, except her own, of course, which was based on her intolerance of humanity with a little Judaism thrown in.

—*Roseanne*

*I*f I really begged her, Nanny would take her teeth out and smile at me. I never saw anything so funny in my life.

—*Carol Burnett*

Each summer my grandmother and I would conspire to indulge her one vice: cherries. She loved cherries. Two or three times a week when my Grandfather was at work, I would walk the mile to the supermarket and buy a half a pound of cherries. My grandmother and I would eat them secretly because my grandfather would have a fit if he'd known we spent an extra dollar a week on them.

—*Geoffrey Canada*

*G*randma counted everything. How many trick-or-treaters came to her door. How many Christmas cards she received. How many pairs of mittens she had knitted. The number of blooms on her prize dahlia. The number of phone calls a day. She kept a green stenographer's notebook where all her lists were tallied by date and year.

—*Teresa Wendel*

I was always happy at Granny Scarberry's home. She was a tiny woman with bright-blue laughing eyes who was fun to be with, and she showered my brother and me with affection and attention.

—*Chuck Norris*

*W*hile I was a child her great affection for me, and her intense care for my welfare, made me love her and gave me that feeling of safety that children need.

—Bertrand Russell,
of his grandmother

he first person ever to notice my music ability was not my father or my mother but Grandma Ada McGill back in Illinois. Grandma, who lived to be nearly a hundred, always remembered your name and recognized something about you, when somebody else might have needed a doggone scorecard to sort out all the children.

—*Barbara Mandrell*

*F*or me, Grandma's room itself was far more interesting than anything outside the window, because it held her many treasures.

—*Eudora Seyfer*

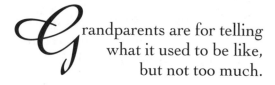

$\mathcal{G}$randparents are for telling
what it used to be like,
but not too much.

—Charlie W. Shedd

$\mathcal{E}$arly one New Year's Eve morning, just after my seventh birthday, I watched my grandmother as she prepared the traditional holiday delicacies. It took hours to make the paper-thin pastry sheets needed for the *spanakopita,* and she'd started at five o'clock, hoping to get it into the oven before the family awakened.

—*Pauline Dimitry*

*M*y grandmother had a reverence for the sun, a holy regard that now is all but gone out of mankind. There was a wariness in her, and an ancient awe.

—*N. Scott Momaday*

*S*he is the only person I have ever known who could make the rain, lightning and thunder go away just by lighting a candle and praying La Magnificat.

—Elisa A. Martinez,
of her grandmother

*W*henever we had to visit Granny at Marlborough House, we always felt that we were going to be hauled over the coals for something we had done.

—*Princess Margaret*

*M*y grandmother had principles of her own. They were the principles of one who was old and God-fearing, who'd lived a life that was upright and hard, full of dignity and honor. Changing her life in any way whatever was the furthest thing from her mind.

—*Svetlana Allilueva,*
daughter of Josef Stalin

$\mathcal{M}$y grandmother often said,
"Learn to write . . .
because it is a piece of bread."

— *Yelana Knanga*

*W*henever I'm having slacks shortened or a skirt hem taken up, I look down at the tailor and see Grandma Becky kneeling there, straight pins between her lips, asking me to turn.

—*Davida Rosenblum*

*I*n our pine cupboard,
Grandmother's
Haviland china, pure white and fragile
as eggshells, rests side by side with the
choicest pieces of my mother's beloved
blue willow. When I look at those
dishes, as I often do, I remember both
my grandmother and my mother—
women who wasted no time "grieving
over what is gone forever."

—*Eudora Seyfer*

*T*his is more nostalgia. The continuity between my grandmother, my mother, and myself is beached on that island. I have an image of a girl fishing from a shaky pier, wearing a big straw hat—and it could be any one of us.

—*Julie Rigby*

Bibliography

Robert Andrews, ed. *The Cassell Dictionary of Contemporary Quotations.* London: Cassell Wellington, 1996.

Robert Andrews, ed. *The Columbia Book of Quotations.* New York: Columbia University Press, 1993.

Robert Andrews, ed. *Famous Lines: The Columbia Dictionary of Familiar Quotations.* New York: Columbia University Press, 1997.

Christina Anello, comp. *For Grandma.* New York: Peter Pauper Press, 1992.

Tony Augarde, ed. *The Oxford Dictionary of Modern Quotations.* New York: Oxford University Press, 1991.

Betty Baum. "Great-grandparents to the Rescue." *New Choices for the Best Years,* Sept. 1991.

Anne Bernays. "Grand (parent) Expectations. *Town & Country,* Dec. 1996: 136–7.

Mary Biggs, ed. *Women's Words: The Columbia Book of Quotations by Women.* New York: Columbia University Press, 1996.

Joyce Butler. "Grandma's Sunday Dinner." *Yankee,* Jan. 1992: 23.

Geoffrey Canada. "Cherries for Grandma." *New York Times,* 13 Feb., 1995: A19,

J. M. an M. J. Cohen, eds. *The Penguin Dictionary of 20th Century Quotations.* London: Viking, 1993.

Karen Cooksey. "Love Takes More than Words." *Modern Maturity,* Dec.–Jan. 1990 : 41.

Gretchen B. Dianda and Betty Hofmayer, eds. *Older and Wiser.* New York: Random House, 1995.

Pauline Dimitry. "Making New Year's Pie." *Yankee,* Jan. 1995: 12.

Stephen Donadio, Joan Smith, Susan Mesier, and Rebecca Davidson, eds. *The New York Public Library Book of 20th*

Century American Quotations. New York: Stonesong Press, 1992.

Eugene Ehrlich and Marshal De Bruhl, eds. *The International Thesaurus of Quotations.* New York: Harper Books, 1996.

Helen Exley, ed. *To My Grandmother with Love.* New York: Exley, 1994.

Robert I. Fitzhenry, ed. *The Harper Book of Quotations.* 3rd Edition. New York: Harper Collins, 1993.

Susan Ginsberg, ed. *Family Wisdom: The 2,000 Most Important Things Ever Said About Parenting, Children, and Family Life.* New York: Columbia University Press, 1996.

Mary Gordon. "The Important Houses." *The New Yorker,* 28 Sep. 1992: 34.

Mary Taylor Gray. "Nana's Cookbook." *Ladies Home Journal,* Mar. 1996: 214.

Dee Hardie. "A New Theater Dynasty." *House Beautiful,* July 1994: 116.

Dee Hardie. "Traveling with Grandchildren." *House Beautiful,* Nov. 1991: 174.

Dee Hardie. "Two by Two." *House Beautiful,* March 1994: 195.

Juwan Howard. Interview. *Jet,* 22 May 1995: 46–7.

Margaret Jarvis. "Don't Call Me Grandma." *Essence,* May 1992: 92.

Valerie Kack-Brice, ed. *For She Is the Tree of Life: Grandmothers.* Berkley, California: Conari, 1995.

Marjorie P. Katz, ed. *Pegs to Hang Ideas On.* New York: M. Evans and Company, 1973.

Chaka Khan. Interview. *Jet,* 16 Sept. 1996: 32–6.

Kathleen Kilgore. "The Suffragette's Dress." *Yankee,* May 1991: 144

Corinne Azen Krause. *Grandmothers, Mothers and Daughters.* Boston: Twayne, 1991.

Janet Lanese, *Grandmothers Are Like Snowflakes. . . .* New York: Dell, 1996.

Carol Spenard LaRusso, ed. *The Wisdom of Women*. San Rafael, California: New World Library, 1992.

Leslie Li. "A Walk Through Nai-Nai's Garden." *Gourmet*, Sept. 1991: 104.

Claudia Limbert. "The Grandmother Who Could Do Anything." *House Beautiful*, Feb. 1992: 8.

Rosalie Maggio, ed. *The Beacon Book of Quotations by Women*. Boston: Beacon, 1992.

Rosalie Maggio, ed. *The New Beacon Book of Quotations by Women*. Boston: Beacon, 1996.

Demetria Martinez. "Our Parents' Parents as Vital Signs for Our Times." *National Catholic Reporter*, 27 Mar. 1992: 16

Rona Maynard. "Improving Ties with Grandparents." *Chatelaine*, Apr. 1992: 38.

Honor Moore. "Grandmother, the Empress." *The New Yorker*, 25 Mar. 1996: 60.

Tillie Olsen, ed. *Mother to Daughter, Daughter to Mother, Mothers on Mothering.* Old Westbury, New York: The Feminist Press, 1984.

Elaine Partnow, ed. *The New Quotable Woman.* New York: Facts on File, 1992.

Elaine Partnow, ed. *The Quotable Woman, 1800–1981.* New York: Facts on File, 1982.

Karen Payne, ed. *Between Ourselves.* Boston: Houghton Mifflin, 1983.

Gaye Rizzo. "'Grandma Comes to a Branch Library: A Foster Grandparent Makes Her Mark." *American Libraries,* Oct. 1991: 904.

John Rosemond. "Grandparents: Important Players in Raising Children." *Better Homes and Gardens,* Dec. 1996: 91.

Anthony and Sally Sampson. *The Oxford Book of Ages.* Oxford: Oxford University Press, 1985.

Jilann Sevenson. "Crafts from Grandmother's House." *Better Homes and Gardens,* May 1994: 94.

Eudora Seyfer. "Behind the Parlor Door." *House Beautiful,* Jan. 1995: 18–20.

Jason Shinder, ed. *Eternal Light.* New York: Harcourt Brace & Co., 1995.

Joyce S. Steward, comp. *Quilting: Quotations Celebrating an American Legacy.* Philadelphia: Running Press, 1994.

Amy Tan. "My Grandmother's Choice." *Ladies Home Journal,* Oct. 1996: 192.

Judith Timson. "Nanny and Me: A Journey Toward Love and Affection." *Chatelaine,* June 1994: 24.

Jessica Treadway. "A Grandmother's Gifts." *Glamour,* April 1995: 286.

Teresa Wendel. "Things that Count." *House Beautiful,* June 1996: 192.

Lois Wyse. "The Way We Are." *Good Housekeeping,* July 1992: 204.

A Grandmother's Journal. Philadelphia: Running Press, 1996.

Grandmother: A Personal Journal. Philadelphia: Running Press, 1994.

In Praise of Grandmothers. Philadelphia: Running Press, 1993.

Mother's Love. White Plains: Peter Pauper Press, 1996.

The Quotable Woman. Philadelphia: Running Press, 1991.